IT COULD BE VERSE

Will Stevens

THE BLUEBELL PRESS

32 Lowther Road Wokingham Berkshire RG41 1lD

© Will Stevens 2012

A catalogue record for this book is available from the British Library.

ISBN 978-0-9531192-6-4

Typeset by The Alpha Xperience, Newbury
Cover design by Philip Hodkin
Printed in Great Britain by TJ International Ltd., Padstow.

'Poetry should be a source of pleasure'

WILLIAM WORDSWORTH

UPS AND DOWNS

Smile

Don't shout at the waiter
It's just not his fault
If the chicken is tough
And the peas are too salt.
He's been here all day
And his feet hurt like hell,
So give him a smile
And then wish him well.

Don't bark at the shop girl
She can't answer back,
And she knows if she did
She would soon get the sack.
It's been a long day
And she's not very well,
So give her a smile
And then wish her well.

Don't growl at the postman
If he's a bit late,
And he's always on guard
For the dog at the gate.
He's been in the rain
For a very long spell,
So give him a smile
And then wish him well.

A smile is like sunshine,
It lightens the way
And flushes out shadows
That can darken the day.
So make it a habit
If your meeting won't gel,
Just give them a smile
And wish them all well.

The Runner

Pigtail flying in the breeze
She strides along with sumptuous ease.
With healthy flush and glowing skin
She runs as one who means to win.

Who is this golden girl of pace
Of slender frame and sunburnt face?
She of the legs so long and strong
With rhythm like a dancing song.

Her lithesome form so skimpy clad,
Can make a lonely watcher glad
And feel that if he raised a hand
She'd flash a smile and understand.

Arrival

We were taken by surprise
At the time that he arrived,
A little quicker off the mark than we had thought.
We were happy with his size
And he otherwise complies
With all the things that make a good report.

He's now firmly in command,
And with everyone in sight
We've got a sudden epidemic of the drools.
He's got hair upon his head,
And he looks so finely bred,
And has the natural air of one who rules.

Very quickly mum and dad
Are slightly up the pole,
As they float about the place in half a trance.
He just lies there on his turn
And sucks upon his thumb,
And contemplates how he will make them dance.

Summertime

A summer smile
Lights up the river bank
Where children play,
And picnics show a wisp of smoke.
Here is plenty, nature's gifts
Lie scattered in abundance
As eager ducks tread water,
Looking for their share.
A flash of blue from dragonfly
And worldly cares unnoticed slip away,
As drowsily we just enjoy the day.

Seaview

A seaside place, no more, no less.
Small, a few shops and hotel,
Where flapping halyards cast their spell.
As to weather -who can guess
What turn of tide will bring?

Walk, early morning, up the hill,
Past the villas brickly red.
Buy the papers and new baked bread.
Sailors dressed against the chill
Soon to contest in the bay.

Linger by the boat strewn roadside,
Wave to friends down on the hard,
Check the forecast at the boatyard.
Small hand tugging, patience tried,
Turn for home and something fried.

Isle of Wight

Another England lies offshore.
A sailor's land.
Where poets wrote in treasured verse
And monarchs came to stay.
Guardian to England's southern seas
This island stands secure
Beyond the narrow straits
And Solent's shipping lane,
As shield to Portsmouth's naval might.
This Isle of Wight, this diamond patch,
Lies suntouched in a restless sea,
Where beaches guarded by stern forts
Preen to the sound of childhood's pleasure time,
And busy are the boardwalks of Ryde pier.

My Friend

My friend asks for everything.
It isn't very much.
A walk, a bed,
To see he's fed,
A kindly word and touch.

He has a way of sitting
That really says it all.
His eyes alert,
His ears pricked up,
Just waiting for the call.

Yes, my friend makes great demands,
Although he knows it not.
Or am I wrong
And does he know
That it's my love he's got?

Maitre'd

His jaw is firm, his eyes are bright,
His dedication clear to see.
His word is law, that's only right,
And comes of being Maitre'd.

His brow is knit with endless care,
His presence drenched with gravity.
He can command with just a stare,
As well befits a Maitre'd.

He welcomes guests with sumptuous grace,
His presence borne impressively.
With dignity he sets the pace,
He is a proper Maitre'd.

Sometimes, oh my, oh quelle horreure!
A commis spills the hot gravy.
A snap of fingers is the spur
For help to come via Maitre'd.

When all is done and tables cleared,
A lonely figure there will be.
His shirt undone, no longer feared,
He's just tomorrow's Maitre'd.

Royal Wedding

Trumpets, let the fanfares soar,
The Crown is riding by,
With gracious wave and smile so sure
To heed the distant bells.

Soldiers, stand your scarlet ground,
The Crown is riding by,
In pomp and majesty profound
To share a nation's joy.

Nobles, wear your splendour bright,
The Crown is riding by,
The symbol of a nation's right
To continuity.

People, raise your flags and shout,
The Crown is riding by.
This is your day to talk about
When cynics have their say.

Reflections

Once is was a place where lives were led,
Joy was felt, tears were shed.
Now it's just a crumpled pile
Of broken brick and old clay tile.

Once it was the scene of family's prime,
Homework done, trees to climb.
Now, the family's gone away,
And memories in ruins lay.

Once it was a place where people laughed,
Loved the warmth, felt the draught.
Now the whisper of the leaves
A wistful mix of mystery weaves

Hired Waffler

From the jungles deep in newsland
Comes a figure, strength displaying,
(Biggest byline, all are saying),
On her way to feed the monsters
Lurking in the murky shadows,
Slavering for their daily fix
Of scandal, mayhem and some dirt.
Inquisition is her business,
She is famous for her quizness.
At her entrance strong men shake
Hoping she a smile will make.

Steely huntress, media queen,
Girt about in skins of splendour,
(Has a husband who's big spender)
Armed with arrow pen and sharp look,
Hypnotises poor defender,
Then fires dart of loaded questions,
Huntress to her Actaeon prey.
Questions finished, arrows quivered,
Leaves her quarry who has shivered,
Then retreats before drums cease
Urgent calls to file her piece.

What is a Clown?

What is a clown?
Someone who laughs when he is sad?
Who lifts you up when you are down
Who makes you say -oh, he's a lad.
But 'though he has the funny clothes,
The wig, the hat, the big red nose,
It calls for something deep inside
   — a special drive
That makes the whole thing come alive,
That is a clown.

Who is a clown?
Good clowns are always far too few,
There's always room for someone new,
It could be you — or you — or you,
If you could bring yourself to see
That awful fool, that loon, that's me.
If you could show that sense of fun
   — that golden thing
That makes the whole world want to sing,
Then you're a clown

Eton Dorney

Olympics 2012

A northerly today,
The flags are streaming hard.
A steely sunshine threads the cloud,
And waves command the course.
The crews begin to make their way
Watched by a well wrapped crowd.

Pull away, pull away, pull away,
Move as one with a rhythmical flow.
All together we'll strive to succeed,
Together we'll show we can stay.
Heave away, heave away, heave away,
Bound as one by a mystical tie.
Together we'll strain every nerve
And we'll fight to make it our day.

This man-made gem;
This water course supreme,
Where matching elegance with scale
Brings lifting of the hopes
That here, where oarsmen play the dream,
Is where they cannot fail.

Stadium

Olympics 2012

This catchment of all hopes and fears;
This pit of cruelty and tears,
Well featured in the glossy mags
As Coliseum of the age,
Where youth, with eagerness and skill,
Will lie defeated in the dust,
While others fly on winged feet
Secure in triumph's sweaty grasp.
The golden touch will fall on some
While crowds in acclamation rise.
Which ever way the coin may spin,
The stadium will always win.

The Angler

He sits, unmoved by wind or rain,
His world a measure of split cane.
His crumpled coat and shabby hat
Drawn tight against the climate's play.
His eyes intent on rippled face
And where a float bobs in its place.
This is his world, where he is free
From everyday and commonplace.
Where he can taste the fleeting bliss
That comes to those who live the dream.

Wendover

Secure in Chiltern's tight embrace,
With thatch on roof and chalk strewn walks,
The village is a tidy place
Where well-clad folks can congregate
For garden club and thoughtful talks,
And there live at a slower rate,
And never watch the village clock
To mark the time it takes to reach
The monument atop the hill.
There, views across the placid vale,
With gentle slopes of oak and beech,
Subdue the sharp red claws of war
And memories of its bloody trail,
While obelisk records it still.

Noise

Monster!
You creeping horror of the age,
You guzzle on your monstrous feast
Of blatant, blaring, grasping noise,
Like some gigantic, slavering beast,
You Minotaur of sound.

Hooligan!
You squalid wrecker of our peace,
From boom and clatter of machine,
There is no refuge, no escape,
And roar of traffic in between,
Makes sure you get your way.

Tyrant!
Trashing our quiet and civil calm,
To cast your brutish, frenzied rage,
And spread your mindless, troubled harm,
And lock us in a quiet-proof cage,
You demon of the mind.

Monster!

PC

I am not politically correct
Whatever that may mean.
I hold the right to personally select
What I do and how I do it,
And with whom I may be seen.

I am not politically correct.
I will not heed a drum
That beats conformity to class or sect,
Nor will I mouth the platitudes
That the chattering classes hum.

I am not politically correct,
And never will conform,
Or heed the call to mentally erect
A barrier to liberal thought,
Or wall of prejudice and scorn.

I will never be politically correct.

Rally

The rape of London's measured beat
By inflamed heads and marching feet,
Throbs to a sense of justice lost,
So break the laws, and damn the cost,
Let's defame statues of men gone,
And defile those who made us strong,
The streets will echo we must fight,'
To keep those things that are our right.
So, rally all, you bright young things,
Black out the cry that reason brings.

Demo

Come on, let us demonstrate,
And remonstrate.
We can show the world a light
And stand up for our human right.
We're young and free
And so should be
The vanguard of the fight.

Let's pitch our tents on public space,
We human race.
And fight against the monster, greed,
That sows its ever growing seed
We're young and bright
And have the sight
To see what must be done.

Don't listen to official cries,
Just turn our eyes.
We don't want unpleasant sights,
Or hear about their legal rights.
We're young and strong
And never wrong
And we can change the world.

The Beat

Life beats to the sound of marching men,
Husband, son and brother.
A conflict finishes, and then
There soon will be another.

Life beats to the sound of fife and drum,
And skirl of pipes of war.
And reasoned voice is stricken dumb
By those who are so sure.

Is there no voice so loud and strong,
To make the clarion call
To show that man's almighty wrong
Could pressage mankind's fall?

Fear beats to the sound of marching men,
The sound of marchers lost.
The battle is just, they cry; but then
The people count the cost

Johnny on the Floor

I saw Johnny on the floor
His body twisted, legs awry,
Arms outstretched to helpers reach,
As classmates in their upright frames
Encouraged him to move — to try.
Then he saw me, gave a smile,
Lifted up a crooked hand
As I met his lifesome eye.

From his strangely crumpled frame
There was a message — 'I will fly,
I've a light to bear me off
And take my mind to boundless realms
Where knowledge is a clear blue sky,
And stars are for the seeing.'
Johnny on the floor is scarred,
But he has a lifesome eye.

The Church

It's different now.
No organ crashes out triumphant ring,
No choir in surplice white, and red.
A different tune is what we sing
By guitar, flute and keyboard led.

Where has it gone?
The church we knew, so confidant and true,
With vicar robed, and Common Prayer.
A treasured place from which we drew
Our lessons in the need to share.

It is still there.
Our church, but fashions ever changing ways
Are not denied in youthful minds,
And liturgy must mark the days
With verities and change combined.

Dreamer

Happy the man who dreams the dream
And sets his spirit free,
To soar above the platitudes
And clichés of the time.

Happy the man whose eyes can see
Beyond the browns and greys,
To the colours of life's palette
There waiting for his brush.

Happy the man whose dream goes on
With every passing year.
He is content just to travel
With no plans to arrive.

Remembering

Wish not for the things that are past
They are but the scenes in a play,
And you were just one of the cast,
By chance who were playing that day.

Dwell not on the things that have been
And try not to think: ah, but when!
Yearn not for the times of your youth,
The world has turned over since then.

Sigh not for the times when you loved
And the beauty that held you in thrall.
Time burnishes images past,
Your present is sum of them all.

The Sea

You, cold sentinel of our land, you sea,
From Dover's cliff you are a stage,
Where sailboat ballerinas dance,
And in carefree pirouette see
Tranquility in your restless swell.

You, calm defender of our isle, you lake,
You can be silently aloof:
Yet give your surface up to ships
Who, flagged and peopled, stream their wake
Across the timeless moat of our defence.

You, rough warden of our homeland, you waves,
You guardian of a people's hopes,
With change of mood so often seen
And sound of cannon as storm raves,
You are the barrier to freedom's foe.

You, girdle of our island home, you deep,
To solid rock and beach you wash,
In ceaseless energetic watch
And everlasting vigil keep,
In preservation of our treasured lands.

It's a Small Country

There is difference, plain to see,
And is no like for like.
Between the southern spaniel
And the Yorkshire tyke.

The tyke is plain in speaking,
With charm in short supply,
But dogged in his purpose
No one can deny.

Broad acres are the county,
Broad character the man.
He breathes air of moors and dales
That mark broad Yorkshire's span.

He doesn't find it easy
To hear the southern view.
Something just as mad to him
As Yorkshire rose turned blue.

There is difference, clear between
All Yorkshire and the rest,
And if tha 'argues down 'int pub
Tha'll see who comes off best.

Getting Wed

Getting wed?
What a lark!
Today you will generate spark,
That will become a blaze
Of many lovely things,
To light the way
Along life's ever testing maze.

Here's to you,
Lovely pair.
May there be good for you to share,
With which, the happy sound
Of unity and fun,
Will show the world
The joyous treasure you have found.

Up North

Stone built and certain in its ways,
This handsome northern gem
Has many treasures to unfold.
With waters of the Spa,
And famous Harlow Carr.
This toffee kingdom of renown
Has charm, and is a flowered town
By moorland crag and rock,
Where special brews of wind blow hard
Across the greensome Stray,
Where Harrogate's own beat
Is marked by well shod Yorkshire feet.

A TOUCH ROMANTIC

Secrets

Who is the girl with the soft blue eyes
As cool and clear as summer skies?
She with the tumbling hair so fair,
Fresh as the breeze of morning air.

Who is the girl with the gentle smile,
And curve of lips so free from guile?
She of the happy, carefree way,
She who can make a golden day.

Who is the girl with the gentle touch
Whose clasp of hand could mean so much?
She of the tantalising gaze,
Is there a hint of wayward days?

Oh, you girl with the soft blue eyes,
I envy him who ever tries
To plumb those depths so out of view,
And then your secrets share with you.

Love

They are quite still
Their wheelchairs locked as they embrace.
Their corner is in shadow.
I cannot see a face.

But I can feel their love.
So fierce, so angered by their state.
A passion held at bay
By malicious, snarling fate.

They break, I see a smile,
Such rapturous, beatific joy.
His twisted hands reach out,
As she tries to touch her boy.

I look away, ashamed,
Uplifted though, because I see,
Their prison door is open
And they have found the key.

Illusions of Spring

As springtime's fragile, firstborn signs appear,
And silvered breezes stir the perfumed air,
A filigreen of green will cloak austere
And starkling branch and tracery yet bare
With hope; that state where fancies quick and deft,
Like fingers at the loom, a pattern bold
Enough to carry dreams among the weft
Will weave, and stir the senses to unfold.
Then, gentle spring will soon be summer's fire.
This sweet burgeoning will fade away
When buds become the flowers of desire.
But if it is that chance, that quirksome mate
Of circumstance, is only making play,
Then hope must look towards another day.

The Greensoft Years

It's a long time now
Since those greensoft years,
When hopes were always as high as the sky,
And I was a boy without any fears,
And you had a come hither eye.

We're so far away
From those shining days.
With plans in our head for flying so high,
And I was a boy who plotted his ways
And you had a gleam in your eye.

Where has it gone to
That lightly young time?
When everything beckoned — please come and try,
When I was a boy with a ladder to climb,
And you had a purposeful eye.

Remember the time
We kissed in the park?
And hand in hand, romantically sighed,
And I was a boy just making his mark,
And you had a smile in your eye.

Our Tune

The tune goes on,
It's place in memory secure.
Remembering
Who danced with whom,
Who's band it was,
Who sang the song,
That made it sound
As if it was for us alone.

The tune goes on,
It has its place inside my head,
Recollecting
The way you were,
The dress you wore,
The way you moved,
That made me feel
That you were really mine alone.

On Berry Hill

I remember that day on Berry Hill
With my girl
Who laughed and tantalised,
And eluded my thinly shadowed hopes
With dancing steps.
Her twists and turns, with thrown back head
And golden hair, enchanted me until
We reached the stile.
Then caught, her arms were opened wide
And summer's heat enfolded us.
That day on Berry Hill.
I remember it still.

Sonnet

True beauty has the longest lease of all
Born as it is of kindliness and truth.
It graciously responds to rise and fall
In quietitude, without pretence to youth.
In fortunes fickle games of light and shade
It steadfastly rejects the need to wear,
Or turn to use of artificial aid,
For ravages and furrows of dull care.
True beauty has a face that shines a light
Into the darker corners of our ways,
And, having seen, will help us in our fight,
Enriching us with hope for all our days.

Eighteen

Oh sweet eighteen, how I remember thee
Youth's garland fair upon thy brow.
With feet set upon a sunshine path,
The world's bright face to see.

Oh sweet eighteen, fight on to hold the dream
That caught such raptures in its sights,
And ranged across those sunlit shores
When all did kindly seem.

On Getting Married

When the bells ring
When we all sing
When we are together.

We will make vows
We will give bows
We will say forever.

We will kiss then
We will amen
We will make endeavour.

I will find you
You will find me
May we never sever.

Looking

Do you see how he looks at her?
He cannot move his gaze.
Her golden hair, her gentle charm,
A smile that lights the room,
She is his world, his everything,
The sun, the stars, the moon.

Do you see how she looks at him?
She's smitten, it is clear.
His ready wit, his eager eyes,
His rugged, happy way,
He is her dream, her treasure thought,
Her man for every day.

Do you not see they show the truth
Of love's great mystery.
Where everything is as it is
And ever so shall be,
To share the dream that love is all
And love is always free.

Young Man's Fancy

It's a wonderful day to be roving
And sniffing the scent in the air.
It's a wonderful day to be fancy free,
No wonder I want to sing.

It's a wonderful day for some smiling
And casting an eye here and there.
It's a marvellous day and I feel so high
Just like a bird on the wing.

I could kick off my shoes,
Wave goodbye to the blues,
And dance all the way down the street.
I could leap in the air
And without any care
Could kiss all the girls I should meet.

It's a wonderful day to be carefree,
With romance a short step away.
It's a wonderful day to be here. and now,
Yes, a wonderful day to be me

TEA IN THE GARDEN

What is a Garden?

What is a garden?
Is it bore — a chore — with just a score
Of reasons why it should be strictly left alone?
Or is it sport — of a sort — and if we're caught
Will never be a second rating thought?

What can it be? Well,
It's seeds — and deeds — and fighting weeds,
With aching back, and groans, and urging things
     to grow.
But it has worth — my earth — I'll give it birth,
And through the rain and shine shall make it show.

Spring

Spring smiles upon the barren land,
Where winter's hard and ruthless hand
Has laid it cold and bare,
And silence ruled the cruel air.

Soon, dew will mark the early morn,
When its bright jewels the grass adorn,
While birdsong fills the air
And willing buds the trees will share.

Greenhouse Blues

I swept up the glass
From the pane in the roof,
The one that's not there any more.
To add to the pain
It started to rain,
And now it's beginning to pour.
The red spider mite
Is starting.to bite,
And the weevils are having a ball.
The white fly is here
And I very much fear
The peppers are starting to fall.
I can see from the marks
Some cats have had larks
On the bench where young seedlings are.

Tomatoes are dry
And now so am I,
So I'm off to the pub for a pint.

The Rose

How like a cat, the rose.
That fragrant queen of garden balm,
To strike a sweet, come hither pose.
Then, when we are seduced by gentle calm,
Unleash a burst of vicious claws
To cover us in pricks and sores.
How like a rose, the cat.

How beautiful the rose.
How beautiful the cat.

Muck

There's beans all hanging long and plump,
And tatties lurking deep.
Rhubarb's growing by the pump,
And marrows on the 'eap.

The peas is climbing sound and strong,
And carrots they look fine.
And we shall 'ave before too long,
Some muscats on the vine.

The beetroot's up — with any luck,
They'll all be making 'aste.
They're on a bed of farmyard muck,
By 'eck, they'll 'ave some taste!

The Orchard

The orchard was a honeyed place
Where ancient trees bent low
Bore generous gifts,
And steely brambles and old shrubs
Shielded its smiling face.
There, verdant meadow leaf
With buttercups and bluebells massed
A carpet wove for dreams,
Where children climbed and played their games
And made their fief.

Summer

When summer's golden trumpets sound
Their notes of hope and joy,
Starvelings of grim winter's grip
Shall dance in freedom found.
Then strike handsome attitude
To the garden's brilliant heads,
And bow in gratitude.

Tea in the Garden

Cup on saucer, ball on bat,
The sounds of summer, English style.
Tea in garden, soft straw hat;
Sandwiches and scones with jam,
Crusty bread and potted ham.

Mother pours, hands the cups round,
Father wakes up with a splutter.
Dog alert and biscuit bound.
Toasted crumpets, fruity cakes,
Sort that only mother makes.

Ring the bell, the children dash,
Flushed and sweating from the cricket.
Dog is frisking, tail will lash.
Orange squash and currant bun
Fed, we sprawl in summer sun.

Trees

A season's brand to mark their time
Regales these guardians of our days.
They stride the land with sumptuous ease
In winter wind and summer haze,
When oak and ash, chiefs of the race,
Stand tall with cousins, beech and lime.

Uncloaked in winter's glinting bite,
They stand in nakedness revealed
In wonderous form, where starkling branch
No longer is by leaf concealed,
And beauty of a different kind
Is garnered in a sharper light.

When springtime comes they open wide
Their fulsome wardrobe of delights,
And help our wintered spirits rise
To watch as new-born bud alights,
And then on every branch and bough
The leaf and flower of hope provide.

Sweet summer's coat is worn to show
It's place beside the evergreen,
Whose slender presence played a part
As silent witness to a scene
Where bright acers, birch and rowan,
Now join the woodlands fructous flow.

And so to autumn's vibrant blaze
Which carries off the summer's dreams,
And memories of indulgent days.
A time when wildlife homes, it seems,
In trees, where life does just adjourn
Until the end of winter ways.

Autumn

That chillbound message in the air,
A greysome tinge to morning light.
Those old companions who will bear
Witness to new autumn's bite.

A wayward hint of red and gold
Amid the summer's vibrant leaf.
Warns that the season's fleeting hold
Is nearly done, and all too brief.

A farewell toss of flowered head,
The calling in of summer's lease,
Confirms a sense of solstice fled
Away with emigrating geese.

Winter

When autumn colour fades
The trees, denuded, stand.
The darkened skies now threaten things to come,
And gentle mists of sweet and scented hope
Make way for winter's jades.

Then, winter's claws dig deep,
Into the yielding earth.
Now starkling branch does frame the ravaged land,
And darkened frostbound air clouds silently
To clothe the hillside sheep.

Autumnwatch

WITH ACKNOWLEDGEMENTS TO THE BBC

When autumn's golden days are here
A path to knowledge we can steer
For Autumnwatch will now arrive
To show the season come alive.

When smiling Kate appears on screen,
Regaling us with what she's seen,
Of squirrels, deer and bat and rat,
She never seems to wear a hat.
(That's good, because the mind just whirls
When we can see those golden curls).

Then Chris with all his corny gags,
To hide the fact that he has bags
Of proper nous about his work,
On things that fly and crawl and lurk.
(And leaving us all wanting more
Of expert tales of wildlife lore).

Now Martin with his wayward locks,
Delighting in his sudden shocks
And quizzes to defeat the best,
All given with his cheerful zest.
(While keeping one eye on the time
And so avoid a programme crime).

And so to level-headed Jo,
And cameramen and crew and co.,
Now thank you everyone concerned,
For Autumnwatch and so much learned.

THE LIGHTER SIDE

Supermarket Blues

Grim set is the visage
Deep furrowed is the brow.
No sense of joy pervades the scene
The mounting tension won't allow.
This cornucopia of fine things
Can hear no thankful, praising voice
For all the goodies that it brings.
The anxious shoppers torn by choice
Push restless hardware too and fro
In making sure they get the best.
And what about the two for one?
To miss on this is quite a blow.
There's out of season fruity zest
And other wild exotica.
Glittering prizes fill the shelves,
Enough to drive one pottica.
There is no time for smile or jest,
Might just miss the special offer.
The simpler days were far the best
And easier on the coffer.

Help!

The heating isn't working,
The boiler's on the blink,
And furry things are lurking
On crocks piled in the sink.
I'm not so good at cooking
And there's butter on the floor.
Things really ain't good looking
When one comes though the door.

It's once a year she goes away
With the girls to chill,
And while she's busy making hay
I'm dealing with the swill.
It isn't fair, I tell myself,
When now the milk's gone brown,
And nothing's helped when off a shelf
Some flour tumbles down.

I stamp, and shout, and mutter,
Which doesn't help at all.
I slip up on the butter
And have a nasty fall.
I'm getting in a dreadful whirl
And don't know where to turn.
Oh please come home my wandering girl,
I've no pans left to burn.

Exercise

I just thought I'd try Pilates,
I wasn't very fit.
I simply wanted smart ease
To reduce me where I sit.

They tell me that my leg will soon
Uncurl from round my neck,
And that my ballooned ankle
Is not quite a total wreck.

My doctor says that looking back
Gives one a view behind.
Something I will greatly lack
When my neck is realigned.

No, I think I've had Pilates,
It really leaves me flat.
I'll carry on with parties,
I'm much fitter when I'm fat.

To My Ego

Now listen, you.
I'm getting tired of your excesses
They're causing me strong psychic stresses.
You're much too keen to make a stand
And show yourself as something grand.
So ease it off a shade or two.

So cool it, please.
Leave La La Land and it's caresses,
Before they cause some big abcesses.
And neither must we upset Id,
He's lots of quirks that should be hid.
So can we have an ego freeze?

Silly Mid Off

They told me to field at silly mid off.
The skipper said 'do it, keep your eyes peeled,
Unsettle the batsman, give him some chat,
Just as he's tapping the ground with his bat.'

The first to arrive I just didn't see,
But I knew it had come by a pain in my hip.
I wanted to hop but knew there would be
A very sharp look from the skipper at slip.

The second one took me via right handed bat
On a spot just below where I usually sat.
This bowler was fast, a strapping great lad
Who just grinned at me as if I was mad.

The third was a ball that bounded and rose,
The batsman then sliced it right on to my nose.
The skipper then bellowed 'should have caught
        that,
You'd better watch out, or you'll be laid flat.'

Fourth one was lower but popped up quite sharp.
The skipper called 'catch' then started to carp.
And muttered to keeper he thought I was dumb.
I didn't care, I was nursing my thumb.

I didn't have time to see number five
And stopped with my arm a full bloodied drive.
The skipper said nothing, just gave me a glare.
I nodded my head and wished him a pair.

Last of the over was fastest of course,
And came off the bat with rocketing force
With skipper watching I knew I daren't yield,
And next thing I knew I'm stretchered off field.

I'm out of the team now, deep in a trough
Because I said no to silly mid off

Sunday Lunch

Three cheers for the Sunday roast
With all the trimmings,too.
It makes a change from beans on toast,
Or a plate of warmed up stew.

Sit family round the table,
For beef and Yorkshire pud.
Please do it if you're able,
There's nothing quite as good.

There's Uncle Fred; whose face is red
From drinking too much gin.
And cousin Prue who should be wed;
And has a soppy grin.

Then there's brother Jim and wife,
A pair not blessed with charm.
They are always locked in strife,
And usually cause harm.

Unwelcome at the party, though,
Is Auntie Bella's dog,
Who always seems to want to go
To his under table bog.

Three cheers then for Sunday lunch,
It stirs things up a bit.
And if someone throws a punch
It really is a hit.

Bossy Boots

They always seem to be so thin,
The bossy ones, I mean.
It must be just the will to win
That tends to keep them lean.

Of course, they're always very fit,
And never overeat.
With all that energy and wit
You'd think they'd overheat.

Oh no, they're always really cool,
Rarely look dishevelled.
The velvet glove is how they rule
Never are bedevilled.

Where would we be without these sprites
To supercharge the air?
They have to reach these dizzy heights
To show us that they dare.

Surprise

Oh, please tell me if it's true
And you're not teasing me,
When with your winsome smile
You tell me I'm much thinner.
Has something generous tempted you
To go that extra mile?
Dare I hope — dare I ask,
Is it spotted dick for dinner?

Plumber's Mate

My girl is a plumber,
A strapping lass is she.
She measures eighty round the chest,
And thirty round the knee.

She can fit a cooker,
And dig a gas main trench.
She doesn't need a plumbers grip,
Just uses fists as wrench.

When she works on boilers
The house can shake a bit.
Some roof tiles may come tumbling down,
And windows take a hit.

She says 'pooh' to ladders,
To fix a ceiling pipe.
There is no doubt about it,
She is a special type.

My girl is a sweetie,
A large size honey trap.
It's just that I get vertigo
When I sit on her lap.

The Wedding

Hooray! The sun is shining now,
It could be quite a day;
With all the family in one place
And all with lots to say.

The bridgroom's looking very calm,
The best man is quite tense;
He has a rather hunted look
As if he wants the gents.

The vicar has a warming smile,
His handshake is quite firm.
Aunt Fanny's hat is really gross,
It makes you want to squirm

There's Uncle George and Cousin Jack,
Dressed up in morning suits.
While Uncle Cyril makes it plain,
He doesn't give two hoots.

Here comes the bride on father's arm
To strains of something grand.
And takes her place at bridegroom's side
So now together stand.

Their promises of age old truth
Are full of good intent.
And husband and a new made wife
Feel all is heaven sent.

A peal of bells, they're on their way,
Excitedly, we follow.
A wedding breakfast waits for us
And we are feeling hollow.

The best man's speech brings down the house,
The bridesmaids are so pretty.
And now the wine is pouring fast
Everyone seems witty.

Hooray! The sun is shining still,
It has been quite a day.
With all the family in one place
And even more to say.

Punting

Never show off in punt.
It's just not the vessel .
Designed for a wrestle,
Or standing on hands as a stunt.

Mind what you do with the pole.
Don't try to be clever
Or you will just sever
Yourself from a boat on a roll.

Don't muck about like a dud.
It's better to paddle
Than cause a skedaddle
And find yourself stuck in the mud.

No, never play games in a punt.

Missing the Boat

I thought the song that we sang
Was a perfect duet,
But it was all a misapprehension.
Like a ship that is beached
We seem to have reached
A state of romantic declension.

I'm like an orange without the pips,
I'm a golfer who's got the yips,
There's something missing and it's all
because,
I can't get started with you.

I'm like a cherry without a stone,
I'm a doggy without a bone,
There's something lacking and it's all because
I can't get started with you.

I thought that we were a pair
Who would always play fair,
But it seems that your smile was misleading.
Like a race that is run
We seem to be done,
With hope for romance now receding.

I'm like a jockey without a horse,
I'm a sailor who's way off course,
I'm all mixed up and it's all because
I can't get started with you.

I'm like a singer without a song,
I'm an onion without the pong,
There's something absent and it's all because
I can't get started with you.

Misery at the School Dance

LYRIC

With our lovely flowing dresses
And our fetching windswept tresses
We should be pleased with every facet
But we're just a wasted asset
'Cos there are no boys around,
We think they must have gone to ground
Oh bother, boo and misery,
There are no boys for us to-see.

We can dance and we are singers,
We could really be hum-dingers,
But there's one thing sadly missing
No one here to teach us kissing,
We think the boys have run away,
We wish they'd change their minds and stay,
Oh bother, boo, we're in the dumps,
We just feel like a lot of chumps.

That we are ladies you can see
Our polish and our poise.
But none of it is worth two pence
When we ain't got any boys.
Our daily round has gone quite flat
We're awfully tired of female chat,
So help us if you can, please do,
Send us some boys — well quite a few.

In Charge

That she's the one in charge
Is written large
On her unfurrowed brow.
Her tilted chin, her fearsome gaze,
Her pigtail flying free,
She knows that she will rule the days,
And she is barely three.

Fairyland

I'm only a pantomime fairy,
The one upstage left, at the back.
I wanted to be on the flyer
But they said that my wings were too slack.

Oh, I wanted to play Dandini
But was told that I haven't the height.
So, blow me down, they gave it to Pat,
And she's bound to be drunk on the night.

I offered to stand by the curtain
And put on an artistic pose.
Their comments were coarse — oh yes they were,
They're common as muck and it shows.

Yes, I'm just a pantomime fairy,
A stationary, non-speaking part.
For actors of deep rooted passion
It isn't a very good start.

Can't they see that I have the talent
For Shakespeare and Ibsen and Co.?
I'm really just made for the classics
And playing the lead in a show.

But I'm just a pantomime fairy
Upstage with a tear in my eye.
I'll never get on in this Amdram
My wife's the director, that's why.

Sell the Family Silver

Let's flog the family silver
Then have ourselves a ball.
It only sits there, tarnishing,
And is no use at all.
We never use the service
It's mugs all round these days,
And silver teapots just don't go
With jeans and lackadaise.

(We'd better keep the rosebowl,
that's quite old-and the tray that
came from home.)

Yes, sell the family silver!
The cleaning's such a bore.
That awful, smelly, messy stuff,
And dipping, what a chore.
We never light the candles
The smoke gets in your eyes,
And no one has a ciggy now,
It really isn't wise.

(We mustn't lose the creamer, though,
and the photos must have frames)

Oh send the silver packing!
It should fetch quite a sum.
It's money laid up on the shelf,
And that is really dumb.
The napkin rings are out of vogue,
It's paper all the way.
And as for salvers — well, who cares?
We'll use a plastic tray.

(Of course, we'll need the cutlery
and the claret jug we'd miss)

Throw out the family silver!
Let's spend it all on us.
No one will notice that it's gone,
There'll never be a fuss.
The social functions that it graced
Have simply had the boot.
So, sell it up — yes, sell it up,
We really need the loot.

(We'll have to keep the sauceboats
though, they're Georgian, of course)

Oh, blast the family silver,
It's been around so long.
We really can't get rid of it
It simply would be wrong.
So shine it up to look like new,
That stuff we nearly sacked.
Then we'll have a glass or two,
To celebrate the fact.

THE THAMES

The Thames

Sweetly flows the Thames.
This silvered carrier of dreams
And history's dark reflections,
Has birth in bubbles in a field
In Gloucestershire; then gently streams
And quickly gathers force
To flow through England's treasured lands,
In witness to the sturdy aims
And hardy stature of its people,
To proclaim a water's course with fate
From placid reach to Traitor's Gate.

The gentle swanspath of the upper reach
Is guarded by the rural calm
Of meadow lands and rush-bound banks,
To dream its way to Lechlade.

A golden stone built Thameside town
 Where church, well known by poet's verse,
Stands tall to dominate the sight.
And with the handsome Ha'penny Bridge
Where navigation starts,
 Lechlade is a town of great delight.

The rivers Leach and Thames combine
At St. John's Lock, the first on Thames.
With ox-bow bends to set its course,
The river's character is set
By Old Father Thames in stone,
Re-sited from the source.

Meandering then to Oxford where they teach,
And is joined by the Cherwell at the spot
Where Christchurch meadow spreads its verdant
balm.

A city with a pretty face
And honeyed buildings full of grace,
Where learned Dons spend fruitful days
By coaching students in their ways.
A swish of academic gown,
Establishes the right renown.
Here is professor so and so,
There, bustling students to and fro.
With Magdalen Tower and its park.
Punt on the Cherwell, what a lark!
Here youthful doors are opened wide
In Oxford, scene of civic pride.
All have a care for Great Tom's peal,
This pretty face with core of steel.

From Oxford south to Abingdon,
And its junction with the Ock.
Passing Nuneham Park and Radley,
Then eastern bound for Culham
With its Cut and science block.
And now turn west and then to north,
For Clifton Hampden's bridge by Scott.
Days Lock lies round a hairpin bend
In shadow of Sinodun Hills,
With tortured bends to Shillingford
With Benson and its airforce spot.
And on to Roman Wallingford.

The stone bridge strides across the land,
Then, with five steps it leaps over the Thames
Into ancient Wallingford.
With brick and flint and lattice spire,
Its history of sword and battle fire,
Define the troubled years.
But ancient Boroughs find their strength in perpetuity,
And here beside the gentle stream
There is tranquillity.

After Goring's beauty of the gap,
And twin Streatly's college barge,
We reach the place where Mole and Ratty rule
And Pangbourne has its famous naval school.
Then to Reading's red brick town
Where cousin Kennet joins the widening stream,
And campus toilers work to dream the dream.

Great beauty in this town is hard to find,
Modernity has cut the ties that bind
To Victorian frills and fancy work,
Now left in solitude on roof to lurk.

When redbrick was the mark of Brunel's age,
Two rivers gave this place a vibrant style,
That struggles for survival in the face
Of hi-tech bustle and commercial drive.
The Kennet, now an urbanised canal,
Twists and turns its way through office land,
While past green meadows and smart river banks
The Thames continues on its placid way.

A campus life, bright star in Reading's crown,
Continually evolves, as does the town.
With theatre and the muses well assured,
This is a town where history is stored.

At Sonning's bridge, eleven arches long,
Languid willows drape their lustrous fronds,
And dinner parties make their way
To where a mill is welcoming the throng.
Then to Shiplake where Tennyson was wed,
The quietest stretch of all, it has been said.
On to Wargrave's black and white,
Marred by traffic, but shielded from great harm
By Hennerton, a secret way of charm.
Then the glamorous Henley reach,
Where the annual row fest tops the bill.
A festive town of great renown,
Henley reigns in queenly splendour.
From Marsh Lock to Temple Isle
Sporting boaters get their fill.

Where Oxfordshire meets Berks
There lies Henley on the Thames.
A town quite used to prominence,
With Festivals and Theatre,
And Regatta's blazered larks.

From Shiplake up the stream,
And Temple Island down,
The boaters throng the waterway,
On pleasure bent for some, while
Sweating rowers chase their dream.

A sculptured bridge the link
Of Remenham to town.
With Upper Thames and Henley clubs,
Then Phyllis Court for croquet,
And Leander's clubby pink.

For those just passing through
Go by the Floral Mile,
Where cheerful trees and verdant swards
Point the way to countryside,
And Oxford's dreaming view.

Now, through regatta's famous mile,
To Hambledon, a jewel of Chilterns Bucks,
With canooist testing weir race
And white weatherboarded mill.
Historic Hurley waits downstream.
A galaxy of islands
And England's oldest inn set seal
Upon this Thameside dream.

The river bends north east for Bisham
And its Abbey, now a sportsman's dream.
And bends again to bring Marlow into view.
A smartish town with handsome bridge,
Whose filigree suspension lends
Elegance to a strong poetic past,
With Frankenstein ranked high among the cast.
Past Quarry Wood of Wind and Willows fame,
And Winter Hill, a viewers favoured rise.
Then past Gibralter Islands for Bourne End,
With sailing club and smart marina
For those with craft of bigger size.
Past Cockmarsh on the starboard side is
Cookham.

An old lady with an aristo air
Cookham nurses a colourful past.
None of its neighbours can ever compare
With the colours it nailed to its mast.
For Spencer the great, its very own son,
Brought greatness and light to this place,
Where church, the river, and much ribald fun
Were part of a great artist's base.

To Cliveden's lovely reach and wooded slopes
The prettiest of the river's many joys.
A famous house of no great age,
Yet cloaked in history's exotica
And tales of many skittish hopes.
Then Boulters Lock, so favoured in the past
By the flappers and their boys.
And two bridges, a handsome one of stone
At end of tree lined banks and built to last,
And Brunel's masterpiece, the Sounding Arch,
Of soaring brick built span for trains to
     Maidenhead,
Where corporate lust has raped Edwardian charm.

High fashion marks the reach to Bray,
Where gastronomes have meeting place
And famous people come to stay.

Bray broods quietly on a raffish past.
Once the hub of fashion's brittle ways
Its black and white gentility
Fits comfortably in modern days.
Now, clothed in timeless elegance
And gastronomic fame,
The church bells peal its history.

Thunder of the motorway and widening stream
Mark Windsor's royal river.
Past Boveney and racecourse, to the town
And its greystone castle,
Dominant protector of a people's claim
To their place in England's living dream.

A town of scarlet finery
And marching bands of cheerful sound,
Great Round Tower and riverside
Where tourists abound.
A place where history is writ large
On castle, church and park;
With cobbled streets and sentry box
And theatre down the hill,
A Borough known as Royal,
As is the peoples will.

Briefly north to Romney Lock,
And bend again with Home Park in the loop,
For Albert Bridge.
A busy stretch; Old Windsor on the right,
And Wraysbury on the left, to mark a quicker pace
And open gates to history's bed of rock,
Runnymede and Magna Carta Island,
Where royalty had changed its face
And Englishmen had seen the light.
Past Bell Weir Lock and racous motorway,
Then under Rennie's bridge of worth,
For Staines, where Richard's sale of fishing right
Established London Stone as boundary.
Then south through Penton Hook and many boats,
And Laleham, Matthew Arnold's place of birth.
Again a motorway disturbs the peace.
When Chertsey's little town is reached, the turn
      is east,
For Shepperton and Walton,
Passing Pharoes Island in mid stream
A nation's gift to Nelson,
The admiral supreme.

North-east now, through urban land,
Past the Molesey's and green Bushey Park,
Then turn again, south-east, for Hampton Court,
And history's red brick gem.
This palace of varieties and home of kings and
    queens,
For five hundred years was for pleasure sought.
Then great bend to Kingston on the Thames
Where Saxon kings were crowned,
And Galsworthy and Gibbon found
Their fame by literary means.
Past Kingston Bridge and Stevens Ayot,
For Teddington's three locks which separate
The upper Thames from widening tidal stream.

Past Strawberry Hill of Walpole Fame
And Eel Pie Island's tangled past,
To Richmond with its hill
And home for war tom fighting men,
Who never will be strong again.
Then under London's oldest bridge to Kew.
History strides the river here with Syon House
On northern bank, and Kew Gardens on the south.
Palace and exotic plants three hundred acres fill
For plantsman's pride and peoples view.

Now, London's river serpentines to east.
Strand-on-the-Green of Georgian taste,
To Mortlake, Barnes and Hammersmith,
Where Bazalgette's suspension bridge,
Whose decoration is a feast,
Stands firmly in mid course of rowers making
    haste.
History crowds the mind as Chelsea comes in view.
Pensioned red coats and two bridges set a seal
On this highly favoured stretch, where art and
    science
Did throughout the years congeal,
Brunel and Turner, names that Chelsea knew.
Vauxhall, Lambeth and Westminster,
Three bridges mark this stretch,
Where government sits in gothic pile,
And broods upon the world from Thorney's Isle.

Past Victoria's embankment to Blackfriars.
The southbank with its theatre and its hall,
Face across the stream to Temple and Savoy,
Then Scott's three arch bridge at Waterloo.
This is the stretch with London's grandest sights,
With London Eye to view Wren's spires,
And to the City where they build so tall,
With bridge to mark Millennium,
And Bankside's arty flights.

London's river is the river's crown.
Rich in its past and pageant's gown.
Witness to savage thrust and noble deed,
With ocean's salt and river's weed
Together, free of locks and weir,
A waterway of life for wharf and pier.

From London Bridge and monument to fire,
A quicker pace, with Tower Bridge in view.
Through Pool of London, quieter now,
Where once it was a crowd of docks,
And Dickens' work was full of shocks.
St. Katherine's now a home for yachts,
While busy shoppers throng the trots,
As emasculated Belfast rides at ease
Under Tower's sullen gaze.

Bermondsey and Rotherhithe and Deptford
Lead the way to Greenwich and the Isle of Dogs.
This once-upon-a-docklands stretch
Is now athrob with commerce,
With buildings taller than the rest.
And city airport of the best.
But, for all that's new and energised,
The eye is caught by Greenwich on the south,
With Cutty Sark of clipper race,
Royal Naval College and Queen's House.
Silent trophies of an empire's place.

Up Blackwell Reach
To pass the crouching monster O2 at the point,
And on to Woolwich north and south,
Where seven silver towers mark the Barrier,
Guardian of London's lands
Against a troubled Thames.
Here the wider river quickens pace;
A marsh filled wind is in the face.
Then under Dartford Bridge, the river's final
cross.
Northfield Hope to Tilbury's busy port,
And Gravesend facing Tilbury Fort.
Now the Thames has shown its range.
Running through the spreading marshland,
The estuary its chrysalis of change,
From placid stream to timeless surge.
Past Sheerness and the Maplin Sand
Submission now to restless urge.
It has a meeting a meeting with the sea at Nore,
And then the river is no more.

Index